This book is dedicated to Alice, Darcie, and Paulie,
with enormous gratitude—"one more time."

First edition 1994

Library of Congress Cataloging-in-Publication Data

Horenstein, Henry.
My mom's a vet / by Henry Horenstein.—1st ed.
Summary: Describes a week in the life of a woman veterinarian
through the eyes of her daughter who assists her.
ISBN 1-56402-234-X
1. Veterinary medicine—Juvenile literature.
2. Women veterinarians—Juvenile literature. [1. Veterinary
medicine. 2. Women veterinarians.] I. Title.
SF756.H67   1994
636.089'069—dc20   93-24964

10 9 8 7 6 5 4 3 2 1

Printed in Italy

Candlewick Press
2067 Massachusetts Avenue
Cambridge, Massachusetts 02140

My Mom's a Vet

by Henry Horenstein

CANDLEWICK PRESS
CAMBRIDGE, MASSACHUSETTS

**I** was trying to concentrate, but Elmo kept nuzzling against me and making me laugh. Baby donkeys can be really funny. I looked over at Mom. She was holding Elmo still so that I could listen to his heartbeat with the stethoscope.

My name is Darcie and my mom is a vet. Vet is short for veterinarian. Mom's job is to drive around to different farms to take care of large animals, like cows and horses. This summer I'm working as her assistant every day for one week. Then I get to go to gymnastics camp. That was the deal we made last summer.

Mom says she's trying to teach me about responsibility and caring for animals. She also wants me to see how she makes our living. I tease her a lot, saying that all she does is play with animals all day while I do the hard work, which is gym practice and homework. Of course, I know she works hard to support us. She starts her day early in the morning, after the bus picks me up for school, and often doesn't get home until dinnertime or even later. I already know a lot about what she does from the stories she tells.

For example, I know that farm animals must have an exam before they can be sold and moved out of the state. That's why Mom and I were seeing Elmo. He was going to Wyoming, but he couldn't be moved until he was certified healthy.

All I could hear through the stethoscope was *lub-dub, lub-dub, lub-dub*. This meant that Elmo's heart was strong. We took turns counting the heartbeats. I counted for a minute and got sixty-one lub-dubs; Mom counted sixty-four. Close enough!

While Elmo squirmed and rubbed against us, Mom and I managed to examine his eyes, lungs, intestines, and heart. We also checked out his legs and feet; then we took his temperature and looked at his teeth to make sure they were properly aligned.

Elmo was in perfect health. He was also bored with us and drifted off to find *his* mother. Mom showed me how to fill out the proper certification forms, and we sneaked away so Elmo wouldn't follow.

om never knows exactly what her day will be like because animals can get sick at any time. A vet has to be available twenty-four hours a day. While some appointments are scheduled weeks in advance, many are unplanned. She'll often get emergency calls either at home or on the cellular phone in the pickup. She even wears a beeper so she can be reached when she's not near a phone.

On Tuesday morning, the phone rang while we were eating breakfast. Paulie Haggis was upset about Sleepy, her favorite riding horse. Sleepy had gone lame. That means she was limping, which is very common with horses. Mom and I grabbed some doughnuts and milk, quickly changed, and drove to the Haggises' farm to see what we could do. It took us about fifteen minutes, just long enough to eat.

Sleepy was a funny name for such a frisky horse. Even with a bad leg, she kept jumping around. I've been around horses all my life, but none as nervous as Sleepy. I didn't want to get too close. A nervous horse couldn't care less who it steps on or knocks down.

Mom told Ms. Haggis to trot Sleepy toward us. We watched Sleepy's head as she trotted. When she landed on her left foreleg, her head bobbed up. She obviously felt some pain in that leg.

Mom did a few simple tests, like squeezing Sleepy's foot to see if she flinched. She didn't, so the soreness was higher up on her leg. Then Mom flexed her ankle for thirty seconds and watched her trot again. This made Sleepy limp even more, which meant the problem was in her ankle.

Mom decided to take X rays to pinpoint the problem. I went to the truck and brought back the equipment. Mom put on a lead apron for protection, just like my dentist does when he takes X rays of my teeth. I stood at a safe distance behind Mom, away from the X rays and away from Sleepy, in case she started to jump around.

Mom took a picture of Sleepy's ankle. The ankle is sometimes called the fetlock joint. Then we processed the film on the spot—it only took about five minutes—and looked at the results.

"It's the sesamoid bone," Mom told Ms. Haggis. "A repairable fracture luckily, but it needs to be put in a cast. We'll wrap it now and send Sleepy to a large animal hospital. They're better equipped to apply the cast. Don't worry. With a cast and rest, she'll probably heal well enough to be ridden in three to four months. But she'll have to be a good patient and stay still."

"Fat chance," I said, as we left Ms. Haggis and Sleepy. "It'll take a body cast to keep that horse still."

Mom laughed and said maybe I ought to assist only on animals smaller than myself.

"Funny," I said and made a face. But not a bad idea when you think about it.

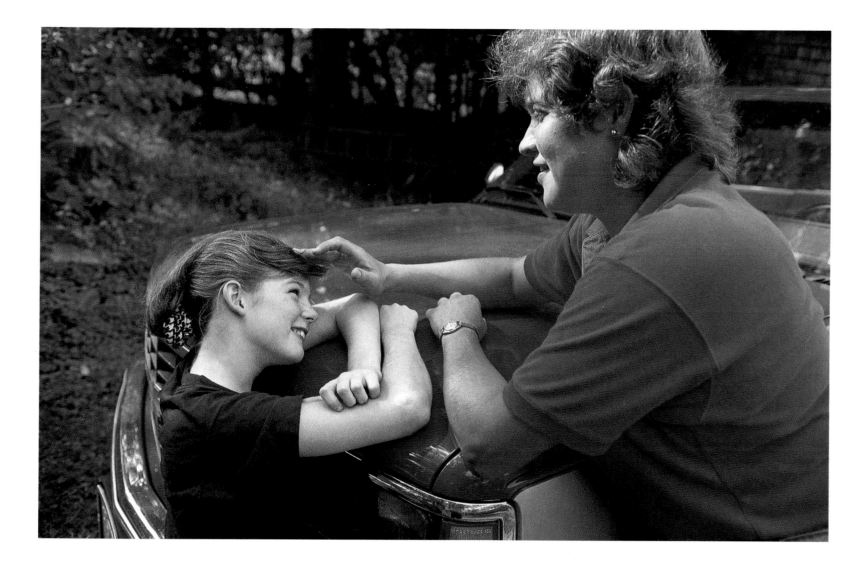

ednesday I got to help deliver a calf! We had a nine o'clock appointment to do some routine cow exams at Mr. Ingraham's farm. On the way I fell asleep because it took almost two hours to get there. That's not unusual. Vets in the country spend a lot of their time driving around, because farmers often live far apart and there aren't that many vets around—at least not vets who know how to take care of goats, horses, and cows, like Mom does.

Mr. Ingraham met us at the barnyard gate.

"As long as you're here," he said, "you might as well help me pull a calf. The cow's having a little trouble giving birth on her own."

Mom and I unpacked the truck in a hurry. We put
on our overalls and boots, so we wouldn't get dirty
in the cow pasture. Then we filled a bucket with
soap and water, took some equipment from the
truck, and ran to the pasture. I kept slipping in the
mud and manure. Good thing I had my boots on.

I could tell that Mom was happy I was getting to see a calf born. Vets rarely help at births unless there's an emergency. Like most animals, cows know exactly how to give birth on their own.

This particular cow had been struggling for a while, probably because it was her first calf. Looking closely, I could actually see two of the calf's hooves sticking out.

Mr. Ingraham was following the cow, trying to catch her, but she kept moving away from him. Mom walked around the cow to guide her toward Mr. Ingraham, so he could catch and halter her.

If she felt a nose first, that meant the hooves were front hooves and the calf was in the normal position for birth. If she felt a tail instead of a nose, that meant the hooves were hind hooves and the calf was in the wrong position. It's really hard for a backward calf to come out, because its rear end is too big.

Mr. Ingraham brought over calving chains. These look a lot like normal chains except they are made of stainless steel, which is rustproof and easy to clean. Calving chains are used to help pull calves out when the mother cow is having trouble giving birth on her own. Mom and Mr. Ingraham placed the chains loosely around the calf's ankles, which were just barely showing.

Mom washed her hands thoroughly, so she wouldn't pass any germs to the cow. Then she put on an obstetrical sleeve. That's a rubber glove used for helping with a birth. It's sort of like the ones you use for washing floors, except it fits all the way up your arm.

Mom told me to grab the cow's tail so it wouldn't be in the way. I wasn't so sure about that. What if the cow got scared and knocked me down?

"Let's find out if these are the front or hind feet," Mom said, as she put her arm up the cow's birth canal. "Good. It's a nose."

"Don't worry, Darcie," Mom said. "This cow's too busy trying to get her calf out. She won't even know you're there."

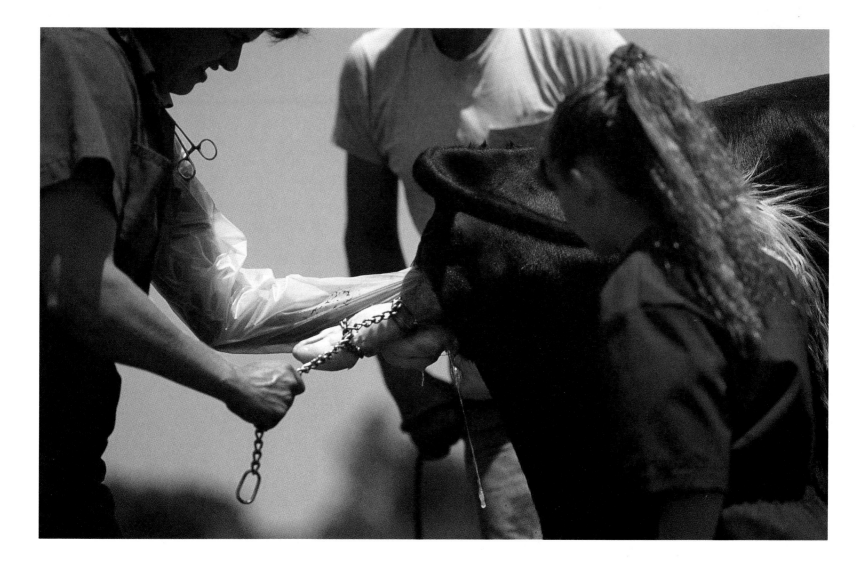

I leaned forward and grabbed the tail. It was muddy and slippery. I swung it to the side and watched while Mom and Mr. Ingraham pulled on the chains. I couldn't believe that my mother could pull so hard. She was even stronger than Mr. Ingraham!

Slowly the calf started to come out. The cow looked pretty calm. I bet she hurt a little but was so relieved that her calf was coming out that she was willing to put up with the pain. That's how Mom says she felt when I was born.

The whole birth took only about five minutes once Mom and Mr. Ingraham started pulling, but it seemed a lot longer. The calf was a bull, which is another name for a male. A female calf is called a heifer.

As he came out I could make out all of his features—his legs, his body, his head. He was all scrunched up and surrounded by placenta. The placenta is the sack that holds a baby animal and feeds it while it's in its mother's womb.

I got an iodine solution, and Mom told me how to put it on the calf's navel to prevent infection.

Just after the birth, the mother cow moved away from her calf. At first I thought maybe she didn't like him, but Mom said the cow didn't know what to do since this was her first calf.

Mom and Mr. Ingraham pushed her toward him, and she got the hint. She began licking him all over to get rid of the placenta and clean him up.

We hung around to make sure things were OK. The calf was a big one, which was one of the reasons the cow had had trouble giving birth. Luckily, he was healthy. His mother really seemed to like him by now.

She kept licking him and poking him to get up. He stumbled a few times, but in about half an hour, he was on his feet and nursing. This is pretty amazing when you think that it takes human babies about a year to stand up on their own.

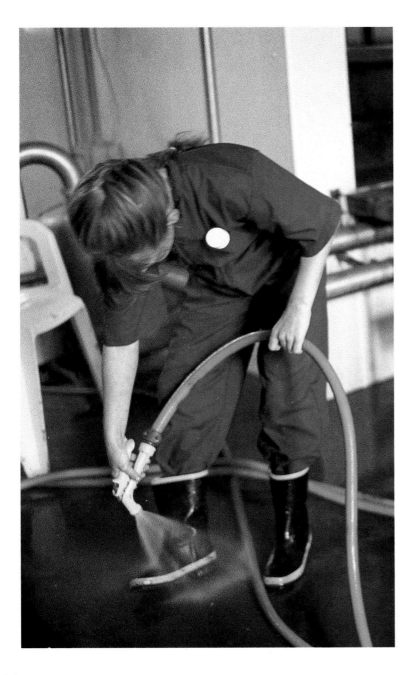

We packed up Mom's equipment and did a few boring cow pregnancy exams on the other side of Mr. Ingraham's farm. Before we left, Mom and I washed our hands and our boots completely clean with disinfectant and water and took off our coveralls. We have to do this after visiting each farm. If we don't, we could carry viruses, bacteria, and disease from one place to another.

I was really tired, but I kept thinking about that calf. I wanted to see him one more time, so we put our boots back on and went to the pasture.

He looked bigger already and was strutting around like nothing had happened. His mother was protective and didn't want me to get close.

But at least I got a few good pictures of him. That way I'll remember my first cow birth.

There were no more appointments scheduled that day, so I got the afternoon off to go swimming and practice my gym routines. But by eight o'clock Thursday morning we were back at work.

ome on, Darcie. We're going to dehorn Billy Bob," Mom said as we climbed into the pickup.

Billy Bob was a seven-day-old goat owned by the Halperins, who live a few miles away. A goat's horns have to be removed early or they get deep into the goat's skull and must be sawed off. Big horns are dangerous because a clumsy or angry goat can butt into a person or another animal with them.

"It's strange," Ms. Halperin said, as we walked over to Billy Bob. "He eats like a pig, but only if we stay with him. He won't touch his food at all if we go out."

"That means he's lonely," Mom explained. "Goats are happiest when they're around people and other animals. If you get him another goat as a companion, I'll guarantee that his food will disappear whether you're around or not."

Billy Bob acted more like a dog than a goat. He
was really friendly, maybe because he was so lonely.
I felt sorry for him. He leaned against me so that
I had to pet him a lot, which I didn't mind doing
at all. And he kept sticking his tongue out and trying to lick me. That was kind of gross but funny.

Mom asked Ms. Halperin to hold Billy Bob and
injected him with a general anesthetic. Before she
gave him the shot, she had to weigh him on the
bathroom scale because small animals like Billy
Bob need less anesthetic than big animals. There's
no way Billy Bob would ever stand still on the
scale by himself, so Mom had to weigh herself
first and then hold him and take their combined
weight. She subtracted one from the other to find
out how much Billy Bob weighed.

Soon after he was injected, Billy Bob closed his
eyes. Then he stumbled around and fell into
a heap on the ground. Fifteen minutes later he
was totally out of it.

I shaved Billy Bob's head with clippers. Then Mom and I bathed the area with a surgical scrub. A surgical scrub is a liquid disinfectant that keeps away infection. I held his head up, while Mom injected a local anesthetic, similar to the kind that dentists use, at the base of his horns.

"The next part looks painful, Darcie, but don't worry, Billy Bob won't feel a thing," Mom promised.

I could barely watch as Mom put a hot iron against his horns. The heat burns the cells that produce horn tissue. Without them, the horns can't grow.

It took only five seconds for each horn. Smoke was rising from Billy Bob's head as the cells burned off, and it smelled terrible. I looked over at Billy Bob's face to make sure he was OK. Mom was right. His horns looked bad, but he was feeling no pain.

When Mom was finished, Billy Bob had a copper-colored ring around each horn. It made his head look weird, like he had an extra pair of eyes. I sprayed yellow disinfectant over the burned areas, so they wouldn't get infected. Then we waited for Billy Bob to wake up.

While we waited, Mom and I made out the bill and gave it to the Halperins. They gave her a check on the spot, which Mom really appreciated. Most farmers aren't paid very much for their milk and animals. They have many more expenses than most businesses. Sometimes they have to wait a month or two to pay their bills. This can make it hard for Mom to pay *her* bills.

It took about an hour for Billy Bob to wake up, even though I kept talking to him and daring him to lick me. He stumbled and fell down a few times, then finally got to his feet and looked around. He was very spacy. It takes a full day for the anesthetic to wear off. But tomorrow Billy Bob would feel like his old friendly self again.

That afternoon we drove almost an hour away to the Hills' farm to take care of their piglets. On the way, we stopped and picked up my friend Théo. She's going to gym camp with me, so we got to make plans while Mom talked to Mr. Hill.

Their piglets were getting really sick because they had been exposed to colibacillosis, which is a bacteria that causes bad dehydration and sometimes death. The only thing you can do about it is to vaccinate the sows, which is what the mother pigs are called, so that the piglets will get protection when they nurse.

When Mom and I got into the pigpen, they followed us everywhere. It tickled when they chewed on our boots, which they did whenever they could catch us. It's a good thing we wash our boots before leaving each farm!

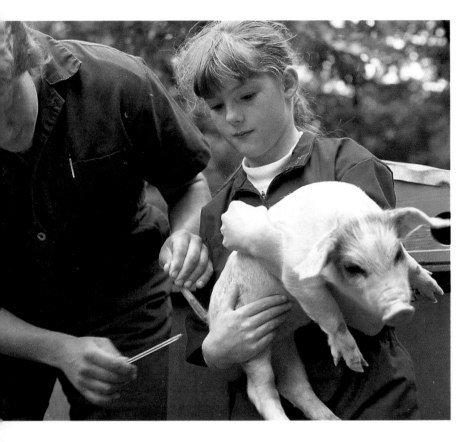

Piglets are tiny, so you'd think they'd be easy to hold. Wrong! They squirm like crazy, and they're slippery. Plus they squeal so loudly that your ears ache when you hold them, which makes you want to put them down in a hurry.

But I finally figured out how to hold them with both hands so they'd be calm when Mom took their temperatures.

Next she injected them with a vaccine to prevent pneumonia and roundworms. These are diseases that a lot of baby animals get.

When Mom was through, she went to talk to Mr. Hill and call her answering service. This gave Théo and me a chance to play with the piglets for a while; then we practiced our gym routines.

"Let's hurry," Mom said, as she hung up. "The Donovans called about Lucky, and I don't think we're going to like what we see." Mom sounded upset. It was obvious something bad had happened.

We washed and packed up. Fortunately Théo's house was on the way to the Donovans' farm. We dropped her off, and I promised to call her at the end of the week before camp started.

The Donovans met us at the pasture gate and explained that Lucky had suffered some eye damage and couldn't see very well. *Some* eye damage turned out to be an understatement!

Lucky was standing around and munching hay when we arrived. He was dark chestnut in color, and from a distance he looked small—not too pretty, but very gentle. When we got close enough to see his bad eye, I had to look away. It was a mess—like someone had punched him.

I had never met Lucky, but Mom had told me a lot about him. For a backyard horse, he was always getting himself into some kind of trouble. Last month he'd twisted his ankle by stepping in a hole. That's when Mom started to call him Unlucky Lucky.

"This came from a blow to the head," Mom told me, after she had examined Lucky. "It's hard to know exactly what happened. Maybe he fell into a fence. Most likely he got tangled up in a rope and hurt himself trying to struggle free."

Animals often get hurt because their owners neglect them or don't know the right way to care for them—like in Lucky's case. Tethering a horse on a long rope to graze is a sure way to get it tangled up. A lot of times owners don't treat wounds in time, and sometimes they even accidentally starve their animals because they don't stick to a regular feeding schedule.

I get really sad when this happens. People should pay more attention to how they treat their animals. A big part of being a vet is educating people who own animals. That's why Mom spends so much time talking to owners when she visits. But there wasn't much she could do to help Lucky. His eye had slipped down on his face and he'd probably never see out of it again.

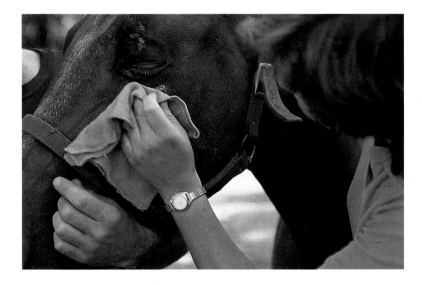

Mom took a sample of the bacteria on the wound with a cotton swab, put the sample into a container, and refrigerated it. Then she cleaned the wound with a disinfectant. Later, we would send the bacteria sample to a lab for testing. The results of the test would help Mom decide what other medication to give Lucky.

Mom prescribed an antibiotic so that Lucky's eye wouldn't get infected. She also left painkillers to keep it from hurting too badly and ointment to help the wound heal. Then she covered Lucky's eye with netting so that insects and dirt couldn't get in.

Mom didn't say very much while she was taking care of Lucky. I could tell she was sad, because she usually tells a few jokes when she works. She doesn't usually get upset when an animal she has treated gets sick or even dies, because it's her job and she's used to it.

But it's another matter when an animal gets hurt because it wasn't treated right.

While Mom gave instructions to the Donovans, I patted Lucky's neck and told him he would be OK, even though I knew he probably wouldn't be.

riday was my last day working with Mom, and it started out routinely. We examined a few pregnant cows and cleaned up a leg wound on a goat. We went home at about three o'clock to celebrate the end of our week and had just changed out of our workclothes when Mom's beeper went off. She called her answering service on the cellular phone and I could tell by her voice that we weren't ready to quit yet.

"Dinner will be a little late tonight, Darcie," she said. "One of Jim Norton's cows is having problems." I was hungry and tired, but a vet's work is never done, as Mom keeps reminding me, so we drove off to take care of the cow.

When we reached the farm, Mr. Norton explained that the cow, whose name was Jenny, had stopped eating three days ago. Cows eat about seventy-five pounds of feed a day—that's as much as I weigh!

After I unpacked the pickup, Mom went to work. First, she took a urine sample, which tested positive for a problem called ketosis. Then she listened to Jenny's stomach with the stethoscope. She snapped her fingers against the abdomen and I heard a *ping* noise, sort of like a balloon when you snap it. That meant the stomach was filled with gas, which was a bad sign.

"It's a twisted stomach," she told Mr. Norton. "The only way to save Jenny is to operate."

Cows actually have four stomachs. After calving, the fourth stomach, or abomasum, sometimes gets turned around so it's in the wrong position. This is almost always fatal if it's not corrected in time.

Surgery is the best treatment and it's commonly done, but it's risky and costs about $175, which is expensive for treating a milk cow. Farmers have to consider whether or not it's worth operating.

If a cow is young enough, in good health, and produces a lot of milk, they'll probably operate. If not, they'll have her slaughtered instead.

"Go ahead and try to save her," said Mr. Norton. "She's a real good milk cow."

Poor Jenny looked so unhappy it was hard to believe that she was good at anything. I was relieved when Mom turned to me and said, "Let's operate, Darcie." But I was also nervous. I had never seen a cow's stomach cut open.

I went to the pickup to get more supplies while Mom injected Jenny with a tranquilizer to sedate her. It took effect almost immediately.

Mr. Norton called a couple of farm hands in to help pull on a rope to drop Jenny down. They tied her front and back legs together and rolled her over on her back for the operation.

I watched as Mom laid out what she'd need for surgery: the gloves and the surgical pack, including all the instruments, sutures, and scalpel blades.

Then I plugged in the light and brought two plastic pails over; Mom sat on one while I stood on the other. That way I could shine light on the surgical area so Mom could see well. The barn was very dark. "This is going to be bloody, Darcie," Mom warned. "It's okay if you want to go outside and practice gym routines while I do the surgery."

I considered it for a second. I hate the sight of my own blood, even when I get a nosebleed. But I wanted to help Mom, and I was curious to see what she was going to do next. I promised I'd tell her if it got to be too much for me.

Mom took the clippers and shaved a large area of Jenny's abdomen. She scrubbed the area clean and made a line with a needle so she'd know where to cut. Then she injected the abdomen with a local anesthetic so that Jenny wouldn't feel anything during surgery.

Mom said that the surgical area must be extremely clean. Any dirt that got into the wound would contain bacteria, which could introduce infection or even cause death.

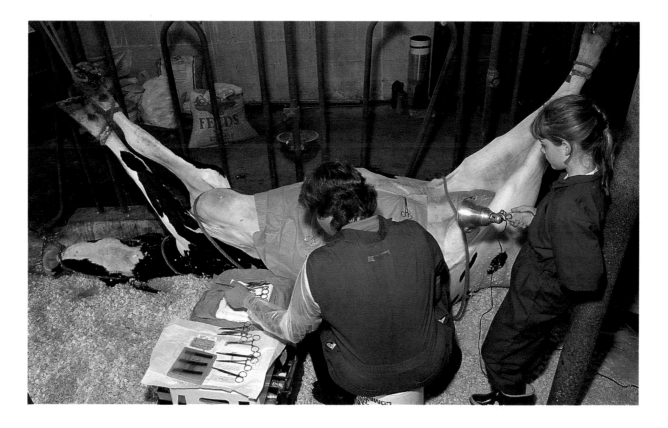

She scrubbed Jenny's abdomen again, then scrubbed her own hands and arms, covered her arms with a plastic surgical sleeve, and put on surgical gloves. She placed a disposable sterile cloth over the clipped area to help keep it clean.

"Now we're ready to cut," Mom said.

I was really getting nervous. But there was no time to wimp out. I had promised Mom I would stay and help. Besides, I knew I could leave if I got sick.

"Shine the light a little higher, Darcie. To the left. Closer. That's it. Perfect. Try to hold it still. Right there."

I concentrated on the light and tried to avoid looking at the trickle of blood that slowly seeped out as Mom made her cut with the scalpel. She had to go through several layers of fat and muscle to get to Jenny's twisted stomach. Every once in a while, she'd hit a vessel, and blood would spurt out like a fountain.

I couldn't believe what came next! Mom put her whole hand right into Jenny's insides and pulled something partway out through the incision. It was the abomasum. She pierced it with a needle, which released the gas, making the abomasum collapse like a flat tire. It's easier to untwist and reposition the abomasum when it's deflated.

Then Mom sewed the stomach to Jenny's insides so that it would stay in place. I felt myself shaking a little as Mom stitched up the stomach area, then the layers of muscle and skin. It took three layers of stitches to get the job done.

Mom asked if I was OK, and I said yes, which was not exactly true. It was really hot and stuffy in the barn, and I was feeling a little queasy. But I didn't want to miss a thing.

"Good," she said, laughing. "You can operate on the next twisted stomach."

This wasn't funny. I was having enough trouble keeping the stupid light steady.

The whole operation had taken a little more than an hour. Mom removed the sterile cloth, and I helped her spray antiseptic all over the surgical site to prevent infections. She and Mr. Norton untied Jenny and moved her so she would rest on her chest until she woke up. If a cow lies flat on her side, she can damage some nerves, and gas can build up in her stomach.

It was time to clean up, so we packed up the instruments and washed our hands and boots.

I was happy to leave the barn. Outside in the fresh air, I felt a lot better.

"Jenny will stand up in about an hour," Mom said to Mr. Norton. "She'll be groggy for a while, but she should be eating by tomorrow."

Mom gave Mr. Norton more instructions along with five days' worth of antibiotics to protect Jenny against infection. Though she could be milked immediately, her milk would have to be thrown away until there was no longer any trace of medication in it.

By the time we climbed into the pickup, it was dark and rainy. I'd completely forgotten how hungry I was.

I was pleased with myself that I hadn't gotten too sick at the sight of blood. It had been a little scary, but it was neat to see a real operation. I couldn't believe what Mom had just done—rather, what Mom and I had just done!

When we got home, I called Théo to make plans for camp. But first I told her about the cow operation in detail.

"Gross! Your mom cut open a cow's stomach? Didn't it make you sick?"

"It's no big deal," I said. "Actually it was kind of interesting."

Acknowledgments

I'd like to acknowledge the many people who made *My Mom's a Vet* happen. The stars of the book are Darcie Haggis; Alice Ennis, D.V.M.; and Paulie Haggis of the Brooklyn-Canterbury Large Animal Clinic in Canterbury, Connecticut. The staff at the clinic included Amy Blakeslee, D.V.M.; Ann Ennis; Evinrude; and Heather Neumann. Théo Thomas played an important supporting role, as did many farmers including Bob Gasparino and Rudy Rzeznikiewicz.

Sarah Durham discovered Darcie, Alice, and Paulie. Mary Lee Donovan at Candlewick discovered the book. Amy Ehrlich patiently shepherded it to completion, with much help from Susan Halperin. Chris Jagmin and Gin Evans contributed the fine design.

There were several able readers along the way who generously offered their counsel. These included Jesse Blake; Shirley Cahill's third grade class at Douglass Elementary School in Acton, Massachusetts; Alex Carrey Cooper; Roy Dow; Diane Grede, D.V.M.; Lori Gustafson, D.V.M.; Julia Hess; Ellie Hollinshead; Pat Hunt; Karen Novak, D.V.M.; Lorie Novak; Elaine O'Neil; and Jacquie Strasburger.

Valorie Fisher spruced up the cow on the cover. And Tracy Hill, as usual, did everything else but take the pictures and write the text. She made all the plans, assisted on location, and was the point person for following up with everyone.

Many thanks to all.